Shattered But Not Broken

By Ticey Windfield

P.O. Box 402
Swiftwater, PA 18370
(973) 348-5067
sspublishingcompany@gmail.com
www.sharsheypublishingcompany.com

Copyright © 2020 Ticey Windfield
ISBN: 13: 978-1-7348030-4-4
Publisher: Shar- Shey Publishing Company LLC
Book Cover Designed by: Dynasty's Visionary Designs
Edited by: ATW Editing

TABLE OF CONTENTS

DEDICATION

I dedicate this book to my three children and unborn grandchildren. **Shattered But Not Broken** is dedicated to every little girl who ever thought that they didn't have a voice. I am speaking for myself and for you. You can finally scream loud and stand tall. I'm your superhero. You are your own superhero. This is for everyone that was raped and left for dead like I was. It is time for you to get up and grab your soul back. I dedicate my book to all of my nieces and nephews, cousins, aunts, and uncles that are walking around with a silent cry. Begin to wipe your tears and stand on your truth. I pray that this book reaches people in our nation that suffered the same walk. My purpose is to break generational curses.

For now, we see things imperfectly, like puzzling reflections in a mirror, but then we see everything with perfect clarity. All that I know now is partial and incomplete, but then I will know everything completely, adjust and say God knows me completely. Three things will last forever: faith, hope, and love and the greatest of these is love. ~ 1st Corinthians 13 verses 12 to 13 NLT

PROLOGUE

I was born on February 14, 1974 to Diane and William Newton in Brunswick Hospital in Amityville, New York. My parents named me Diamond. I was a bubbly baby girl born into this world as most children are, innocent, waiting to explore the world around me. But my innocence would soon be shattered and I would be thrust into a very dark and cold world. I would endure and suffer what no human being should ever have to go through. This journey started thirty-four years ago and it has been a journey filled with winding roads and many hurdles along the way. I would often reflect about my childhood, not understanding why my childhood was snatched away from me. Life was definitely not fair, or at least my life wasn't. The people who were supposed to protect me, dropped me and left me to die among the wolves.

For many years I had suppressed my feelings. I was so chained to my past, I would often ask "why me?" but a few years ago, I stopped wondering "why me?" and decided that it was time for me to heal and to turn my pain into my purpose. Sharing my story is the first step in taking my life back. Living in the past was beginning to eat at my body, mind, and soul and started to affect my relationships with those closest to me. I realize that I had to take the bandage off to allow the wounds to heal. I know that many in my family will not understand, but it's time to break the generational curses and kill them at the root, so they will no longer hold my family hostage. Physically, I am a strong woman, but as the years progressed it started affecting me spiritually and mentally, and all of the different personalities I had used to adapt no longer worked. I was spiraling deeper into my darkness, but that was not good for my immediate family and I could not allow my dark past to destroy my family. I had to finally face what I was running from. I would never have made it without recognizing and coming to terms with what was chasing me.

"Fear of abandonment made me comply as a child, but I'm not forced to comply anymore. The key people in my life did reject me for telling the truth

about my abuse, but I'm not alone. Even if the consequence for telling the truth is rejection from everyone, I know that's not the same death threat that it was when I was a child. I'm a self-sufficient adult and abandonment no longer means the end of my life.

~ Christina Enevoldsen, The Rescued Soul

CHAPTER 1

THE BEGINNING OF THE END

From an early age, my parents made sure we were always busy with housework. "Diamond," my dad would say, "You are on KP this week, and if it's not done right, your ass will get another week." Whenever I heard those dreaded words, it sent lightning bolts down my spine, as I stepped up onto the old milk crate to wash the dishes. Dishes—that was an understatement. In our kitchen, we had pots big enough to feed a prison. If they were not cleaned out immediately, the resident roaches would be all over the place. When they weren't crawling across the counter, getting into my mother's fried chicken lard that sat next to the stove in a greasy ass metal container, (this oil was reused numerous times, after cooking fried chicken, pork chops, bacon, etc., my mom would drain the used oil back into the metal container that was used for months or maybe even years) they were also hiding in the large industrial-sized pans that my parents left soaking for us to wash.

So when it was my turn to wash the dishes, I would climb up on the milk crate because, by the way, I started washing dishes when I was only three-going-on-four-years-old. Just imagine your toddler standing on a milk crate, washing big pots and pans, while fighting off roaches. I would have to use bleach to sanitize the dishes, and I was scrubbing these pots without any gloves. I grew accustomed to balancing myself on the crate, often lightheaded from the stench of the bleach and trying to hold the rag in one hand and the dish in the other. Some might compare this gesture to a ballerina on her toes, in the *releve* position, but I felt like a slave. By the time I was six years old, instead of my hands being baby smooth, they looked like the hands of a sixty-year-old railroad worker. But there were no songs for me; only the sound of my father's voice saying "You're on KP."

I wasn't in this hellhole alone. I had three brothers, one sister, and a cousin JL who lived with us. My cousin's mom had him at 14; she was not ready to be a mom or stop hanging out in those streets, so since my mom was the oldest of all her siblings, she felt like it was her family duty to take him in. As my mom would often remind us, we had just another mouth to feed. My siblings and I were more than enough for my mom. She would often say degrading things to us such as she would tell us that she should have kept the afterbirth, or "I'll send you little fucks to the fucking foster care." The harsh words that she would spit out of her mouth hurt me more than the physical abuse. Her words would irritate me, and I would roll my eyes and she would say, "Bitch you think I don't fucking see you?" She would still have her back turned while yelling at me. She said, "My third eye can see everything. She said, "If I come over there, I'm going to fuck your fat ass up, bitch." I was looked at with such hatred, because by this time she was in my face spitting and yelling and smacking me, screaming, "I can't stand you." So, in my mind, *why in the fuck did you give birth to me?*

We all had chores. My brothers and my cousins were responsible for the garbage, yard work, cleaning up after the two dogs, and cleaning their rooms. They started going to work with my dad when they were eight years old, or I believe it might have been even younger. The physical labor was taught and delegated amongst the six of us at very early ages. We were taught survival of the fittest, first come, first serve. If you missed, that's your ass. They would say, "If your little ass can walk and talk and hold your own bottle, it's time for all of y'all little bastards to earn your own keep. There ain't shit in this world for free. You have to use what you got, to get what you want. Closed mouths and legs don't get paid for free." My mother would say, "Do you hear that, you little bitch?" That word "bitch" cut through me like a knife.

My sister was made to learn and assist the cooking of most of our meals. At a young age, she was made to help my mom prepare three-course meals, which would have been a relief had I not been responsible for prepping the food and washing the dishes. Although I was only seven years old now, I had the bulk of the house chores. I was responsible for washing dishes, washing all the clothes, folding the laundry, cleaning bathrooms, and my bedroom that I shared with my little sister, who at the time was messy. We would have our sister quarrels, because I'm a neat freak and always had a problem sharing my space with anybody; it immediately makes me have mood swings. I was taught the old-school way of cleaning, on your hands and knees, scrubbing with a toothbrush and bleach, and that stink-ass Pine-Sol. We were a family of eight, and there was a large amount of laundry and dishes to keep up with. I felt like my tasks never ended.

We did not have a washing machine to wash. Clothes—oh, we had a washing board. It was literally a pain to wash clothes, as I would crash my knuckles against the groove of the board. My hands were sore and swollen and the skin on my palms started to feel like sandpaper and calluses began to form. My hands were ugly as hell every day. I can remember the worst was the socks. It took a long time to get them clean because they were always filthy.

Although we spent a large amount of time cleaning, the house never seemed clean. My mother was a hoarder and kept a much-cluttered house that was roach and mice infested. She and my father often fought about the cleanliness of the house. Oh, he was meticulous about cleaning and she did not want us touching her shit. Her shit was just junk laying around that she enjoyed collecting. I found myself cleaning around it, which still left the house cluttered. No matter how much we cleaned, it never seemed to get clean.

After our chores were completed, my father would inspect and he was extremely anal about it. He would give it the white glove treatment, and if he found one speck of dirt he would make us redo all of the chores all over again. My house was always the house where people would hang out. My mother would give anyone a hot meal or a place to stay. From the outside, we looked like the Good Times family, but on the inside, especially at night, it was the house of horrors.

I am what time, circumstances, history, have made of me, certainly, but I am also, much more than that. So are we all. ~ James Baldwin

CHAPTER 2

INNOCENCE LOST

Research says that you start to have memories as early as two, but by the age of seven our childhood memories start to fade. But I can remember like it happened yesterday, what happened to me when I was four years old.

I wanted to scream out, and I felt like I was dying. It's funny how at four years old you actually have memories. I wonder if good memories last as long. My trusting nature was going to be my first downfall. He was a man who often came over to our house. I trusted him and never thought he would hurt me. He was Uncle Todd. I always sat on his lap and he would often give me a nickel to buy candy. He would give me attention that I was seeking.

One day, Uncle Todd gave me a dime to get a lot of candy!! I was so excited. He said, "The only thing you have to do is buy candy for me too, and bring it to my house." Now, this may be crazy for a four-year-old, but our small block was a community, or so I thought. We called it a village. The whole block raised you and the people in the community, teachers, principal, were able to beat you with a paddle if you were sent to the office. There was no reason why any neighbor could not spank my bottom or feed me at any given time. I can remember this so vividly that it is scary, because I don't know how I could, only being four years old. I took the dime and ran to the neighborhood candy house to get candy for me and Uncle Todd. As promised, I went to his house immediately after to take him his candy. When I got there, he was watching TV, and it was so strange I remember as a little girl, I was in the living room and he asked me for the candy. I proudly and innocently took some candy out of my pocket and smiled like I had accomplished the greatest feat a four-year-old could. Uncle Todd said, "Good girl, this is all the candy I like, but there is some other candy I like too, but you can't get it with money."

I was so intrigued, even as a four-year-old. What could this candy be? I soon found out that it was something I could never have imagined in my little

mind. He took his hands and grabbed my little hand

and put them on his face and smiled. I remember

thinking I wanted to go home. He then forced my hand

in his pants and I could feel this long, hard thing. Then

he took his hands and put it in my panties. I said I

needed to go because it was dinner time and Mommy

would be looking for me. He said firmly that I was not

going home right now. Then he grabbed me, and I

began to pull away and beg of him to stop. He then

began to tell me what he would do if I tell. I said, "Tell

what? That I took your candy?"

I started kicking and peeing on myself,

screaming, "Stop, it hurts! You're my uncle. Mommy!

Daddy! Please, the monster is ripping my guts out."

17

The room was spinning. I began vomiting. His fucking breath made me throw up in my mouth, while I began to feel this excruciating pain that was unbearable. I began to fantasize that I was a superhero to cope with my abuse. All three of my different personalities, Diamond, Destiny, and Nina, literally saved my life. I thought I would die and everything went black.

When I woke up, I was at home, and Uncle Todd was there. He told my parents that he found me by the candy house and someone had beaten me up and taken my candy. I didn't know it then, but this man robbed me of innocence and at just four years old, I lost my virginity to someone I trusted. This monster was so close of a family friend that we called him "Uncle." This event changed my life. I was too young at that time to really understand what Uncle Todd had done to me, but what I did know was that it hurt and I never wanted to go through anything like this ever in my life. It was the beginning of a legacy of abuse that would alter the entire course of my life. It had a lingering effect that trickled down to my own children, not sexually, not emotionally, sometimes at the hands of others with my unspoken permission. It took away my ability to trust, and my ability to love.

This was my mother's story from four years old. For this reason, she was an extremely depressed woman who allowed her past to control her. Diane, which was my mother's name, was the victim of abuse that started when she was raped at four years old. I sometimes feel very sorry for her because I feel she never had a chance at a good life. But then at other times, I feel you make the decision about who you will be. I realized that back in my mother's time, they hid things like this under the rug. What happens in the family, stays in the house. Secrets many have taken to their graves.

I am not sure if my mother was just a horrible person because of her experiences, or if she had a sense of entitlement because of them. Part of me feels that it was a sense of entitlement because of her horrible past. She felt that the world owed her something. For this reason, it seemed that for many years my mother used my father as a crutch to get through life. She seemed to idolize him. Sometimes my father William would talk down to my mother, and although she seemed to worship the ground he walked

on, there were still times when she would defend

herself. The dynamic was very strange. One thing that

was certain was that he treated her better than any

other man in her life did. She was pretty much the boss

of the house and my father would concede if things got

too heated. He would never put his hands on her or

abuse her physically. My mother catered to my dad

and they seemed to make their relationship work.

Whatever it was, it seemed to work for them.

My parents raised us in a strict household. My

dad was a stern disciplinarian. When he asked for

something to be done, he would only ask once. If you

did not do what he asked, the consequences were dire.

The punishments we received from my father were

very severe. He would beat the boys with cable cords, but not the girls. To discipline us, my mother would beat all of us with cable cords or whatever she could get her hands on. So, although we got a reprieve from dad, my mom kept things pretty even. I, specifically, would be beaten with a wet cable cord by my mother. This added another level of pain that was indescribable.

My father William had other creative punishments for all of us. Like having to jump up and down on the cement floor of the basement until he said stop. We were not allowed to ask if we could stop or he would give us another hour. If you stopped before he gave you permission you got an additional two hours. He would also make us stand for a long period of time

22

facing the wall with our hands behind our backs. If that punishment wasn't strong enough, you were told to put your back against the wall, kneel in a sitting position, then place your hands in front of you as if you were positioning your arms to carry something. My dad would place this big ass Yellow Pages telephone book that probably weighed 10 pounds times countless hours of holding it. If you dropped it, that was your ass. Believe me, you preferred to hold this book, because a beating was serious in our household.

I remember one particular time when my dad made my younger brother stand in front of the wall. Keep in mind, my little brother Anthony had a disability as a result of a prenatal procedure; I believe an amniocentesis test was given to my mom, where a needle went into the front of my brother's skull. He and my sister Sheila are twins. They had this thing they would do where they would move their heads back and forth; it seemed to have a calming effect on them. On this particular day, my father made my brother stand in front of the wall facing it. My brother began to move his head back and forth. We all knew he could not control it, as it was something that just came naturally to him and my sister. My father walked up behind him, grabbed his head, and slammed it into the wall with such force that it opened the wall. My brother just sat there and cried. Our hearts went out to him because we knew he could not help what he was doing. It seemed everyone understood that but my father—or maybe he just didn't care.

My father supported our family as a plumber and electrician—he was also a known con artist. He would sometimes con some of his clients and perform work that was not really needed. This was a testament to his lack of character. He seemed to be harder on me and my older brother than any of the other kids. I remember asking after leaving home why he was so hard on me. His excuse was that he saw something in me that he didn't see in the rest of his children. I told him that meant nothing to me, and it seemed he would have tried to build a more loving relationship with me. I did not understand. As I got older, I began to think that maybe my dad saw more of himself in me and that is why he showed me very little love. He was the first man that abandoned and rejected me, and it was a pattern that I would follow for years, always picking the same type of men.

I don't know if my father was ever in the military, but his obsession with cleaning sometimes made me think so. I kind of wish that he were because that could at least give me something that I could have been proud of. My father was an alcoholic and I can't really remember sharing any touching father/daughter moments with him. My dad was very condescending when he would talk to us, and didn't believe in apologizing if he were wrong. Neither my dad nor mom ever used the word love when we were growing up, so for that reason, I don't know what that look or feels like. However, my dad did equip me with a toughness that I needed to survive out in the world that was about to eat me alive.

CHAPTER 3

PART OF THE GANG

It wasn't just that she missed her friends; she was starting to wonder if she needed them around to feel like she existed at all." ~ Ann Brashare

One summer day, I was doing my regular chores, hoping to get outside and have some fun. After I finished cleaning the bathroom, doing the laundry, and washing the dishes I felt a spark of excitement because I could finally go outside and play. I was always somewhat of a tomboy and could not wait to go out and play with my brother and his friends. It did not matter what the game was. I was down to play football, wrestling, competing in lifting weights, as a superhero like Wonder Woman, any game where you have to be strong, bike riding, etc. I started believing I could do anything a man or a boy could do. I was strong and could always keep up with them. I was so happy they accepted me and allowed me to be part of their group.

There was an older woman that would give the children cookies on the block. My greedy ass decided to eat some of her cookies even though they were stale and I started throwing up. My posse of homeboys began to laugh at me. So, I began to wrestle with one of the boys. I wanted to get the attention off of me and the embarrassing situation I was in. I started getting the best of the boy, and the rest of the group started chanting, "You are gonna let a girl kick your butt!!" This earned me a solid place within the boys' group.

We always had a lot of fun together and sometimes we would get into mischief. One day we happened to stumble upon a toy factory. We looked inside of the windows in awe. We were all very poor and we rarely got toys. We could not believe that there were toys within our reach. All the toys we could carry. Through the windows, we could see dump trucks, guns, and walkie talkies. We dared each other to break one of the windows so we could go inside and take what we wanted. Finally, one of the boys broke the window and we were all able to go in and grab as many toys as we could. We did this frequently and we kept this within our group because this was our own special place. It was so much fun; it was like Christmas every day.

My brothers and I had to be inside before it got dark. My father would always say, "Don't let the streetlight catch you!" My father was a hard man that we did not want to disobey. The consequences would be too great. We came home within seconds of the streetlight coming on. It was always a relief when we were finally in for the day on time. The day had been a wonderful adventure, but little did I know my life would change forever in a matter of hours.

CHAPTER 4

NINE YEARS TO LIFE

In order to escape accountability for his crimes, the perpetrator does everything in his power to promote forgetting. If secrecy fails, the perpetrator attacks the credibility of his victim. If he cannot silence her absolutely, he tries to make sure no one listens. ~ Judith Lewis Herman

As I looked into this shattered mirror, I began to form a clear picture of the girl I used to be. I was Nina until age seven. It was then that I became the victim of yet another predator, my mother's other brother

Dexter. My mom allowed me to spend the night over at Uncle Dexter's. I was woken out of my sleep to yet another uncle destroying my innocent nine-year-old body. At this point, I am numb. I was supposed to be spending some time with his daughter who is my first favorite cousin, although we live in different cities. It's a turn up every time we connect.

Uncle Dexter is no longer alive. There are predators that hunt in the jungle and in the African plains. Those predators fight for survival in an unforgiving world. They have to eat or be eaten. I have a great respect for the strength and the fortitude of the predator that hunts their prey and catches it to feed their families. Unfortunately, the predator I encountered at the tender age of seven was someone who shared my flesh and blood.

When Uncle Todd became a teenager he had to come live with us. I never did know why he lived with us. He started spending the night at our house rather frequently and then he just moved in. My father did not really care for him but allowed him to stay with us because of my mother. For some reason, he was not welcome in my grandmother's house. As time went on, I began to see why. It could have been lack of room there or it could be that he was such a horrible son of a bitch that his own mother could not stand the sight of him. I would vote for the latter.

He would stare at me very intensely and make me feel very uncomfortable and intimidated. It was like a game he used to like to play. It seemed to give him some type of sick pleasure to make me feel the way he did. He knew how he made me feel. I could not hide it, so it was very evident how uncomfortable he made me. While his intimidating stare frightened me, I was still unprepared for the hell I would suffer at his hands for nine years.

Dissociation gets you through a brutal experience, letting your basic survival skills operate unimpeded ... Your ability to survive is enhanced as the ability to feel is diminished ... All feeling are blocked; you 'go away.' You are disconnected from the act, the perpetrator & yourself ... Viewing the scene from up above or some other out-of-body

perspective is common among sexual abuse survivors.

~ Renee Fredrickson, Repressed

CHAPTER 5

THE VISITOR

Over the years, I had suppressed most of my past in a secret, dark place in my heart, but I remembered I started having nightmares about waking up to my uncle's hand over my mouth, telling me to be quiet.

Every night, we finished all of the chores after dinner and then we washed and went to bed. I was very tired from the excitement of the day and welcomed a good night's sleep. I could not tell how much time had passed, but I was awakened by someone touching my body. I was about to cry out for my mother and father to help me, but he put his hand over my mouth to quiet me. I could not believe this was happening again. All I could think was… "Why?"

The first time the "visitor" came into my room, he played with my body, groping, and feeling me up. He touched my chest. I was seven years old at this time, not even developed yet. He ran his hand down my stomach, and as he tried to make his way down between my legs he was startled by a noise in the house. On that night, he was deterred from his filthy intentions, so this time, he left quietly. After he left, I was thinking to myself, "Was I having a nightmare? Was this real?" I was praying that this was a bad dream.

The answer to that question came the next night when he returned. I was asleep in my bed and suddenly awakened by hands roaming all over my tiny body. It was not a dream and the reality of the situation hit me. But this time, he was not playing with my body. He was going further than he did the night before. Who was this person who was in my room so late at night? As I got my bearings, I started to try to stop him from touching me. Who is this? Who could be doing this to me and why? I continued to try to stop him, but he became more aggressive as I tried to fight him off. After what seemed like an eternity, he started to get on top of me and pry my legs open. I locked my legs as hard as I could and then I looked up and saw the face of my nightmare. It was my uncle. My mother's brother. I cannot describe the fear and betrayal I felt once again. I knew who my attacker was. It was not a stranger or a family friend; it was my flesh and blood. Tears rolled down my face and I couldn't believe this was happening to me. He tried several times to penetrate me, but I was too small so he began to spit on my vagina so that he could enter me. He was raping me so bad I saw stars, and felt something pop in my uterus. Urine began to flush out of me. I fought him off the best I could, but he was bigger and stronger than I was. After I realized I could not win this battle, I turned my head and closed my eyes and continued to cry.

It was finally over and I was confused and afraid. My tiny body was ravaged with pain. I pulled myself out of the bed. Because of the intense pain, I was unable to walk, so I crawled past my parents' room and scratched at their door, deathly afraid, whispering, "Mommy, Daddy, the boogie man is hurting me again," but their TV was so loud. There was a rule in our house that until our parents opened their bedroom door, we were not able to knock or bother them until they woke up and opened their bedroom door. I continued to crawl my way to the bathroom.

There was an iron heater in the bathroom that I grabbed on to help pull me up on the toilet. I laid some of my body across it, hoping to get some relief. When I finally made it to the toilet, it hurt like hell to urinate, and blood and flesh and slime came out of my vagina. Just try to imagine the pain of a miscarriage when you are just a small seven-year-old baby.

"I have to get to my mother, my father, sister, someone," I thought to myself. I had to tell them what just happened to me. I froze in my tracks as the event flashed back in my mind. I can't tell anyone. He told me that he would hurt anyone that I told and that no one would believe me. I was a prisoner of this man. There was nothing I could do. I was seven years old, alone, and scared. How could my life be over when it was supposed to be beginning? If there is hell, I am already in it.

After those nightly visits, my personality started to change as I began to find defense mechanisms in order to deal with the hellish circumstances that was now my life. I was trying to make myself forget what was happening to me. My personality began to change and I stopped being a happy child. I was often depressed and in a dark place, and I developed multiple personalities.

Abuse changes your life...Fight Back and change the life of your abusers by Breaking Your Silence on Abuse! ~ Patty Rase Hopson

CHAPTER 6

NO LONGER HUMAN

The molester came into my room almost every night, and each time I felt like he was ripping my insides to pieces. I was so sickened by him until I would vomit in my mouth. The smell of his saliva made me cringe, as he would always spit in my vagina to lubricate it. The more it happened, the more desperate I became to escape this nightmare. After a period of months, I began to fantasize whenever I was being raped. I used to pretend that I was one of the most powerful women in the world like Wonder Woman. Like I ruled the world and no one could hurt me. I would take myself on little adventures where I would catch the bad guys and send them to prison. I had superpowers that would allow me to escape all the villains that were after me. I realized that I did have a superpower. My imagination. It was the only thing that got me through these very trying years.

After about a year, he began to get very comfortable and wanted more than just sexual intercourse. He came into my room, and this night was like any other. I went into my fantasy world and stayed there until he was done. But to my surprise, he was not. He put my face toward his penis and forced me to give him oral sex. Each night after that became worse than the last. He had an animalistic, insatiable appetite for twisted sex acts. He started to sodomize me and

force me to perform oral sex on him on a regular basis.
I started to urinate on myself hoping that it would deter
him, but it never did. I felt dead inside and out, like a
walking corpse. I was ready to die and I wanted to
escape this prison. I felt death would be a welcomed
change. Anything would be better than this.

I began to abuse myself in various ways. I felt
worthless. I began to feel like I was not a human
being. My mom would call me a bitch and slap me in
the face, and my uncle used me as his sex toy with her
permission. My dad did not talk to me much. He
would only talk to me when a task needed to be done
or when he felt I needed to be disciplined. I felt ugly
and insignificant like no one would care if I lived or
died.

On one particular day, I decided I was going to end my life. I could not go on this way. I got some pills out of the medicine cabinet in the bathroom. It didn't matter, I grabbed whatever was there. I knew that no matter what it was, if I took enough of it, I would die. I sat there and looked at myself in the mirror and thought how much I hated my reflection. My heart filled with hate the longer I looked at myself. I started taking the pills. I began to feel very nauseous and dizzy, but I didn't care. I went into my room and lay down and closed my eyes. I hoped it would be the last time that I laid in this horrible bed.

I woke up the next morning and I was extremely angry. I could not believe that it didn't work. Why am I waking up to this life again? I thought to myself that there had to be a way to end this miserable existence. After this failure, I tried several things to try to take my own life. I would take any cable wire or rope and put it around my neck and choke myself until I was so uncomfortable that I had to stop. I made a noose one day and tied it to the door, but that didn't work. My parents began to think I was crazy because I would do things to punish myself, like tying a string around my tooth and the doorknob and slamming it shut so that I can yank my teeth out. I would use any sharp object I could find to make myself feel pain. I would also slit my wrist, but nothing worked. If I didn't have any sharp objects at my disposal, I would use my ten fingernails and dig them in my forehead and scratch myself all the way down to my chin. I would dig deep into my flesh so that there would be marks in my face.

I wanted to look as ugly as I felt. I became addicted to

self-mutilation. I wanted to feel pain. It was the only

human emotion I was capable of and I couldn't get

enough of it. What I didn't realize then was that God

had a purpose for my life and no matter how hard you

try, you can't kill what God has ordained.

Kids don't remember what you try to teach them.

They remember what you are. ~ Jim Henson

CHAPTER 7

MY ONLY SANCTUARY

Although my life was unbearable at home, I found sanctuary at school. I was not an A student by any means. I did struggle, but I never gave up on it. The teachers used to say how pretty I was and how nice my big eyes were and would always ask me why I looked so sad and angry. If they only knew. I used to think that when people gave me compliments it was because they wanted something from me. So, I hated compliments. My lack of self-worth did not allow me to take a compliment or trust anyone. I hated myself. I was always bigger than my siblings and I always had a big ass and big boobs.

Compliments made me uncomfortable and school was the only place I got them. But even with that, I liked going to school. It was my escape from the house and I was happy there. I had friends and I had teachers who showed interest in me. There was one librarian in particular who would reach out to me because she wanted to help me. She encouraged me to keep studying and come to the library whenever I needed to. I was not going to share my home situation with anyone, but it felt good that someone actually wanted me to do well and believed in me. The encouragement from the librarian and the sanctuary she gave me got me through many tough days.

It was Friday, and I was depressed as usual. Most children love Fridays because they have the weekend to look forward to. For me, it was two days that I would have no sanctuary and no one who cared about me. I got home and did my chores and went to my room. I was very angry and antisocial. I did not want to engage with anyone in the house on any level. I hated the house and I hated everyone in it. My siblings would try to reach out to me, but I was having none of it. I did not want to laugh, talk, or socialize with them. So, I just stayed in my room by myself, thinking of ways to put the house on fire or poison my parents and uncle. My fascination became so strong, I started to plot their assassination; revenge was in the making, and they had no idea that I was plotting to end all of them.

CHAPTER 8

AUNT FLOW

"How might your life have been different for you if, on your first menstrual day, your mother had given you a bouquet of flowers and taken you to lunch, and then the two of you had gone to meet your father at the jeweler, where your ears were pierced...and then you went, for the very first time, to the Women's Lodge, to learn the wisdom of the women? How might your life be different?" ~ Circle of Stones by Judith Duerk

I got my menstrual cycle when I was ten years old. It went away for a year and it came back when I was twelve. It has been irregular ever since it started and that had to do with the sexual abuse that I suffered at a young age. These deranged men damaged me physically and mentally.

When I was twelve years old, my mother took me to the OBGYN to put me on birth control pills, but the doctor refused and my mother took me to the clinic and they put on birth control pills instead. My mother told everyone that I was hot in my tail, but the only sex I was having was forced sex. What really hurt was that my mom knew I was being molested by her brother and she was pretending that I was having sex with random people to protect her brother and make sure that he didn't get me pregnant. My mother was really sick that instead of protecting me she was making sure he never got caught.

I still attend the same OBGYN over the years, and last year when I went to her office, before I left I told her that I was writing a book. She asked me what the book was going to be about. I told her that it was about my life and how I survived rape and molestation at an early age. She asked me a few more questions and some of my story began to come back to her. She asked me my mom's name and she said she remembered when my mother tried to put me on birth control and she refused, but she also recalled asking my mom to leave the room so she could ask me questions. She said that I refused to tell her anything and that because I didn't share any incriminating evidence to her, she couldn't call the authorities just based on instinct.

I revealed to her that I was scared because, before we arrived at the doctor, my mother told me that if I opened my big-mouth that she was going to kick a hole in my ass and that I would end up alone in a foster home. She said, "those people are not going to give two fucks about your dumb ass." The doctor's eyes filled with tears and she apologized for not being able to save me, but I told her it was not her fault, I was just too scared to tell anybody.

CHAPTER 9

IS HELP ON THE WAY

When I woke up on Saturday, I decided to try to go outside and play with my siblings and the dogs. Being so closed off was taking a toll on me, so I figured it was time for me to try to live, in spite of the circumstances. My uncle saw me outside playing and I could feel him watching me. He used to look at me in a way that would creep me out, and he would make sexual comments. I tried to act like I did not see him staring at me, hoping that he would leave me alone. Unfortunately, it did not work. He called out to me and told me to come into the house. I was hoping that my brother would notice me leaving, but he was oblivious to my absence.

However, this time there was someone else was watching him. It was my step-Aunt Suzie who was dating my Uncle Jerry. She was watching the interaction between my uncle and me. She heard him call me into the house and she followed us to the basement. She saw my uncle feeling on me and heard him asking me to take off my clothes. Aunt Suzie yelled at him and asked him what he was doing. She said, "I am going to tell her mother." She grabbed me and dragged me out of the basement and took me to my mother and told her what she had witnessed.

"Finally," I thought to myself, "this nightmare is over. Finally, someone is telling my mother. I will finally be able to live my life without this unspeakable abuse."

I was unprepared for the events that would follow. I was shocked and hurt as my mother told my Aunt Suzie that she did not believe her and that I was a "fast-ass bitch who was "hot in the pants" and she didn't believe her brother had done anything to me. I was deflated and confused. I did not know what to do. My mother didn't believe me.

My Aunt Suzie was livid. She told me that I should not have to go through this. She told my mother she wanted me to come live with her. My mother only refused and told her to mind her business. Aunt Suzie was so angry. She went home and told my Uncle Jerry what happened. The next day, my Uncle Jerry came over and beat up my Uncle Todd.

I thought this would deter him from bothering me, but it only made him angry and he abused me even more. The attacks became more violent and torturous in nature. To make matters worse, my mother told me that I better not ever tell my father about what was going on between her brother and me.

The abuse continued for eight more years. I became a bitter, hateful person as a result of all that I had been through. I could not imagine ever being with a man or loving any person. All these years, I had grown up without love and felt it was something that didn't exist. I learned during those years that no one was safe from sexual abuse in my family. Male or female, it made no difference. Everyone was preyed upon. Every time I would think about the fact that I was related to the people in my family, I would feel nauseous. They were horrible people with no morals. I had to get out!

CHAPTER 10

ULTIMATE BETRAYAL

My parents started playing cards with friends and some family members. They would have casual drinks and then it escalated. During the 1980s my father introduced crack cocaine into our lives. Initially, we were very confused about the traffic that started coming into and out of our house. My father would go upstairs for long periods of time with these people and the smell of the smoke would take over the house. When they emerged from the room they would be sweating and their pupils would be so dilated that they looked like owls. They were also very paranoid. This

SHATTERED BUT NOT BROKEN

was funny for a while, but then it just became old,
embarrassing, and pathetic. Money was getting low
and food stamps were being sold for crack cocaine. I
learned later on that my parents were no strangers to
drugs; they used them before they had children. Now
both of them were crackheads.

Our parents were lost in a drug haze 90 percent
of the time. The daily routine was that they would
sleep all day and stay up all night smoking. My father
was a plumber and electrician, but he was not working
because he was either asleep or high. He would get
high all night and sleep all day. My mother would get
high all night but she would not sleep all day like my
dad. She seemed to be lucid enough to try to stick to
daily routines like cooking and raising us, so in spite

of the night before, she would still get up to cook, etc. I looked at her as a functional crackhead. With my dad not working, this left me and my siblings in a situation where we had to make our own money and provide food for ourselves. We were on our own. But I made a promise to myself that no matter what, I was not going to quit school.

One day, one of the dealers that used to hang out at our house came over. He was much older than I was. What I did not know was that my dad owed him a lot of money. My dad did not have the money, so he told the dealer he could have sex with me to settle his debt. I was in the living room watching TV when the dealer approached me and told me about the agreement between him and my father. I could not believe what was happening. My mother told me to never tell my father about my uncle, but now he is selling me for a twenty-minute, twenty-dollar bill? Ain't this a bitch!! I looked at him with a blank stare. I could not believe what I was hearing. My father told me to go with him. My heart dropped as we left the house and went to a cheap hotel. When we got there, he told me to get undressed and get in the bed, so I did. I had no more fight in me and just lay there while he emptied himself on me.

The emotional, human side of me started to disintegrate. By this time, I was numb and I felt nothing. My own father had sold me for a piece of crack!! I kept thinking it over and over in my mind. I lay there and just told myself it would be over soon.

When it was over, he took me home and we never spoke about what had happened on that day. The dealer still came to and from my house, selling drugs to all the people that would come and go as if nothing ever happened.

CHAPTER 11

STRANGER IN THE MIDST

After the betrayal of my father, I was lost. I was lost and angry. Between the ages of 12 and 16, I began to act out and became very mischievous. I started hanging out in the next town over and smoking marijuana. I did it because everyone else did and it also gave me a convenient case of amnesia that would help me forget just for a while what my life was like. I then began to learn the ropes of making money in the hood. I had nothing to lose and I needed to make money. I started dealing drugs when I was 14. I would make a couple of hundred a day, which was not bad for a person my age.

Money was out there to be made and I was down to make it. There was one particular guy who was very thugged-out and bullied everyone. He was also very disrespectful toward females. He would say derogatory things to me but I would ignore him. After hustling one night he offered to drop everyone off. There was a group of us, but I was the only one who lived in the next town over so he was dropping me last. He said he needed to run into his house to get something and told me to come inside with him. I really didn't think anything of it because we hustled together and we also smoked an ell or two from time to time.

Once inside, I became a bit uncomfortable because he wanted me to go into his room. His parents were asleep in the house. We went to his room and with every step, I felt more and more uneasy. We got to his room and he said he needed to plug in his room light. This ugly, fat, scar-faced gorilla walked up behind me and put a gun to my back. He said if I didn't give the pussy, I would be sorry. He told me that I better not make a sound. I started struggling with him and he started pulling on my pants and then my panties. We continued struggling, but he was so strong. He was a beast, an animal, and I could not win. As he raped me, I lay there crying and helpless with tears rolling down my face. He kept saying things to me like he always wanted me and loved my big titties and fat ass. I told him I hated him and he was dating my best friend, why was he bothering me? After it was over, we left the house and went back to the car for him to take me home.

The whole ride back was filled with threats. He told me he would kill me if I told my best friend or anyone for that matter. I started having out of body conversations with myself about how much I wanted to kill him. I felt like just turning the car over and killing both of us. I kept thinking to myself: Kill him!! Kill him!! The voice got louder and louder. I felt like I was going insane. What do I have to live for if the majority of my life was spent being tortured as someone's sex slave? We pulled up in front of my house and I got out of the car. I felt so worthless and disgusting.

When I got into the house, I went straight to the shower to wash the smell of this animal off of me. As I gazed into the mirror, my attention went to the medicine cabinet. I grabbed the first bottle of pills within reach, not even knowing what they were and tilted my head back and started pouring the pills down my throat. While I was in the shower, I began to feel dizzy and disoriented and saw white spots in front of me. I managed to make it to my bed, hoping that I would never wake up. Of course, this was not the first time I tried to take my life. I am thinking now that my life must have been spared so that I could help people by telling my story.

CHAPTER 12

HOMELESS

Because of my parents' drug addiction, the bills were not being paid. The lights and the water would frequently get shut off due to the lack of payment of the bills. Although this was a frequent occurrence, my parents would usually find some way to get the utilities back on. However, as their addiction became worse, they cared less and less about the living conditions. There was also another reason why our house was not taken care of. My father was having an affair and eventually left my mother for another woman. Things really started to fall apart once he left.

We started going long periods of time without lights and water. I did not know what we were going to do after my father had abandoned us; we were desolate.

One day my mother started sending us to different places to live. We were all split up. I went to live with my mother's best friend Pam. Aunt Pam accepted me in her house and treated me like I was her own daughter. I was very comfortable living with her. Although she liked to party, she did not entertain crack like my parents. She was like a Godmother to me and her children were like my siblings. I was so grateful that I had somewhere stable to live so that I could finish school.

One morning, I was getting up and Pam's baby's father came into my room. I shared a room with Pam's son who had already left for school. He told me that I was not going to school that day. I was very confused about why he would say that. He started walking toward me with this horrible expression, and he had these nasty dreadlocks. He is what I would imagine Medusa's son would look like. He was Jamaican and spoke with a heavy accent, so most of what he said I could not understand. But even though I could not understand him, he still gave me the creeps and made me feel very uneasy.

He started coming towards me, saying he had been watching me. He started touching me and I started squirming and I tried to move away. I wanted

74

him to leave me alone. He made remarks about the

way I looked and how he had feelings for me. I started

feeling very nauseous; I thought I was going to vomit.

I started wrapping myself in the comforter on the bed

as tight as I could and begged him not to do this to me.

Tears rolled down my face. His eyes were bloodshot

and he reeked of weed. It was disgusting. He forced

himself on me, and like so many times before with all

the other predators in my life, I was just not strong

enough to keep him off of me. I was uncontrollable

and continued to kick this fucking rapist off me. He

locked his legs between mine and then he was kissing

me and trying to force his tongue down my throat. I

tried to turn my face away as much as I could, but

those fucking dreadlocks were smothering the shit out

of me. I began to wish that they did. He was making a horrible groaning noise in my ear. The voice in my head screamed out that it would all be over soon.

He dropped down on me after he finished. I started pushing him off of me. He grabbed me by the neck and threatened me. He said no one better ever find out about it. He said if I told anyone they would not believe me and he would deny it. He said if I ever told anyone that I would be sorry because he would kill me. I gave him the look of death. I turned over with my guts throbbing and sobbed like a newborn baby. I had no energy to move. I lay there plotting. How would I get revenge on this bastard?

One thing about me: I have an unfuckable, revengeful, spiteful, cold-hearted other side of me. When you do me any harm, I will silently destroy everything you desire. You will never eat off a full plate again, without me helping myself to their riches. Kill and destroy was my mindset.

I kept thinking to myself: "What can I do to get back at this snake?" I was trying to go to sleep and forget what just happened to me. I felt numb and hoped the feeling would never go away. I finally fell off to sleep. Tomorrow was another day and I vowed to myself that he would be sorry. I was done with being a victim.

The next day I woke up and an idea came to me. It was perfect! This motherfucker is going to be sorry and I planned to hit him where it would hurt him the most. See, he was a drug dealer and I knew where he kept his stash of weed. He hid large quantities behind the walls of the kitchen cabinets. I jumped my ass on the counter when he left the house. I grabbed the screwdriver and pried the wood apart and robbed him. He sold it in large quantities. My idea was that I was going to steal his weed. I helped myself to two large zip-lock bags of his marijuana. I made a few dollars and gave some to my cousins who smoked weed. This was not a one-time deal. I started stealing his weed on a regular basis and selling it. He was too stupid to even notice. I felt like I was smarter than he was, and in spite of what he had done to me, I had the upper hand

now. I was raping him in his pocket and the dumb

bastard didn't even know it. This is when I really

started hustling in the streets. I would make a couple

hundred a weekend from his stash and for me that was

what he owed me and then some.

My mind was also trying to find other ways to

get back at him. One day, the opportunity presented

itself. My Aunt wanted us to take a family picture. As

soon as that creep touched me, I cringed. He had his

hand on my shoulder and the look of discomfort on my

face must have been very evident, because my

Godmother asked me if everything was okay. I could

feel him staring at me and I told her everything was

fine. I did not take his threats lightly, as he had physically hurt my Godmother before.

The relationship between my Godmother and the creep was deteriorating. One day, we were talking and the subject of her baby's father came up. I told her that I did not like him. She asked me why I did not like him. I hesitated to answer the question. I was wondering what the consequences would be if I was honest with her about why I felt the way I did. She would not let it go, so I decided to just let the chips fall where they may and tell her everything. I told her I did not feel comfortable because I thought she would not believe what I had to say and would not help me. My own mother and father did not help me, so I felt there was no chance for anyone else to care enough to believe me and protect me.

I started crying and I told her everything. She stared at me because it took me so long to say what I had to say. After I finished talking, I felt she didn't believe me. She just stared at me with a vacant look on her face.

There was a brief, awkward silence and I said, "I knew you wouldn't believe me." She just looked at me.

When she broke her silence, she said she believed me and that she would help me. My god-brother chimed in and told her that her baby's father did things to me and that he was mean to me. I think she was in shock about what she had just heard. She continued to look at me and she became angry.

She called him on the phone and she asked him if he ever touched me. He became very irate. I could hear him screaming at her on the other end of the phone. Before hanging up the phone, my Godmother reiterated that she believed me and no matter what he said, she knew he did something to me and that he was a disgusting liar. When she hung up the phone, my Godmother told me she was there for me and no one would hurt me like that again. I was grateful to her for her kind words and also grateful to her for believing me, however I became very disenchanted because the authorities were never called. He never suffered any consequences for what he had done.

He, nor any of the other devils who had hurt me ever saw the inside of a jail cell. It still sickens me to this day. That decision did not change the love I have for my Aunt Pam. She took me in when no one else wanted me. That speaks volumes, when someone has three of their own biological children and then opens their house and heart to somebody else's problem. I'm very thankful; otherwise, I would have been homeless before the age of 16.

CHAPTER 13
FAMILY REUNION

My mother decided that she wanted all of her children back together. Unfortunately, this was not because she loved us and missed us and wanted a family. The only way she could get help from Social Services was she had to have all of the children back under one roof with her.

We lived in a condemned shack of a home with no water and no electricity. Before we moved in the shack it was inhabited by stray cats with fleas. The house was damaged by fire, the bathroom was completely burned up, and so was the kitchen area.

There wasn't even a stove to cook on. We used a kerosene heater to heat the shack, cook, and bathe. We had one pot that we used to wash ourselves and cook our food. My oldest brother was like a dad to us now that my parents were separated and we were now homeless. He made sure he fed his four siblings before he fed himself. He used to put government cheese, rice, and tuna in the pot, and that was what we would eat. We got water by borrowing the water hose from our neighbor. We draped sheets around the house to create some form of privacy. There were holes in the roof, so when it rained, we all got wet.

There were cat urine-soaked mattresses left in the house that were infested with fleas. This was where we slept at night. My second brother and I were eaten

85

alive on a regular basis by the fleas. It did not help

matters that we were both bedwetters. I became a

bedwetter as a defense mechanism to try to stop my

uncle from molesting me. Sometimes he kind of makes

me wonder if he was a victim too. There was no lock

on the front door of the house, so we would barricade

it with a two-by-four every night before going to bed.

We created a makeshift lock, so to speak. My mother

slept with a loaded shotgun to protect us during the

late hours of the night. We lived in the hood of our

town. The crackheads were out in full force every

night. They would steal anything they could get their

hands on so they could get their next fix.

No matter what was going on, I always tried to

make sure to get some sleep. I had to go to school

every day no matter what. We all wore hand-me-down clothes or clothes from the thrift store. The popular girls at school would tease me about the way I dressed and wore my hair. If they only knew, the clothes I wore were not a major concern in my life. I had so many other things to be concerned about. I sometimes think about those girls and the horrible things they used to say to me. But then I can almost guarantee that I grew up to be the better woman than their mean, trifling asses. No matter where they may be in life, they did not have to travel the road I did. I bet if they did, they would be dead by now. I have grown into an awesome woman and I am sure they didn't see that coming.

One day after school, my brothers and I were getting off the bus. We saw two white men talking to my mother. As we approached our house, we could hear them telling her that she had 24 hours to get us off of the condemned property. They admonished her that this was no place for children to be living due to the condition of the house. They told her the place was scheduled to be demolished that day. But they were gracious enough to give her 24 hours to find someplace else for us. My mom promised that we would not split up. She called one of her friends and asked them for a ride to the Social Services Office. He came and picked us up and we went to the office. We sat there for what seemed an eternity.

My mother was very distraught and crying at first, and then she pulled herself together and promised no foster care, and that we would get through this together. She reminded all five of us survival is all we know, now let's get through this together. She was trying to figure this entire situation out. She did not know what to do or where we would go, and she needed immediate help. The people that worked at the Social Services Office had no empathy for us or the other families that were in our position. I wonder why people get into a profession where they are supposed to help people if they do not care about people. While we waited, they were calling shelters to try to find accommodations for six. This took all day and we were all hungry and tired. They gave us one apple all day. Finally, they found a place for us. It was a welfare hotel/cottage that was located in Hampton Bays. They paid for a taxi for us and we went.

The ride was very long and dark, because it was late by the time we were assigned a temporary placement, until emergency housing was available. There were a lot of woods along the way. I was thinking to myself, "Where in the hell are we going?"

We were very nervous. We didn't know what to expect. The unknown factor of this made me very apprehensive and afraid. My mother was trying to be sure of herself and strong, but I could tell she was nervous as hell.

The taxi took us to the front of the building and my mother got out of the car. We were waiting anxiously in the taxi while she was inside. They gave my mother the keys and told her what room we would be staying in. We took what belongings we had into the room. We were all nervous and tired and went to sleep. The room was large enough for all of us to bunk together. With it being very late, there were no other people out and it was very quiet. It felt very spooky to me. I was so scared.

We realized the next day that we were not welcome there because of the color of our skin. We were awakened the next morning by noises from people screaming, talking, and chanting. We did not know what was going on. We looked outside to see what the noise was. There were men with white sheets on their faces. They were chanting, "Get out of our town niggers!!" They started to hammer a wooden cross into the ground in front of the cottage and wrapped a cloth around it. They tied a noose and hung a black baby doll from it and tied it to the pole. Then they poured gasoline all over it and set it on fire.

I felt so disrespected. I remember seeing movies with these types of things happening, and I could not believe this was really happening now. I felt there should have been something that we could have done. They were getting away with murder as far as I was concerned and there was nothing we could do about it. It felt so weird that this was still going on. I studied Martin Luther King, Harriet Tubman, and Rosa Parks in school and learned about the civil rights movement. I was in utter disbelief that during my lifetime something like this could happen.

The cottage superintendent called the police and told everyone to stay in their rooms. When the police came, they made them leave but did not make an arrest. The police left and we all worked together to put out the flaming cross. After it cooled, the superintendent cleaned up the mess. Unfortunately, that was not the only racist incident that took place in the Hamptons.

It was time to go to school. I felt very nervous and upset after the cross burning, and I was so unsure about what to expect at school. I went to bed, and when the next morning came we prepared for school.

We all got dressed and went to wait for the bus which stopped right in front of the cottage. The bus pulled up and the driver opened the doors. All the children on the bus were white and they were all screaming at us. They were saying, "You niggers are not getting on this bus!! We don't want you here!!" We did not ride the bus that day; the superintendent took us to school.

The trouble with the bussing continued until my mother went to the school district and complained. She told them she was going to call the media and expose the Hamptons for the racist place that it was. That was the last thing they wanted. After that, we rode the bus but it was never a pleasant ride. Daily, day-to-day in school was also torture at the hands of racism. I did not learn a thing. I was spit on and called names on a daily basis.

One day, my middle brother who had made the wrestling team got into an altercation with another boy at the school. The wrestling coach came to get me at dismissal so he could get me and my brother out of the school safely. The wrestling coach had taken a liking to my brother Jarrod and tried to look out for him, but he realized things had gotten to a very volatile point. He knew that if given a chance, someone would really hurt my brother. Jarrod has the strength of Hulk Hogan, but if they were to jump him like they wanted to, he wouldn't have survived that fight. Those good ole boys played for keeps.

When he got us back to the cottage, he talked to my mother and told her that it would be best for us to leave the school.

My mother told Social Services about the issues and racial tensions of the Hamptons and all the things that happened, from the cross burning to the bussing to the school situation, and they agreed that they needed to find a more suitable place for us. We did not return to Hampton Bays School. Within that week they found somewhere else for us. The Ronkonkoma Inn was another emergency welfare hotel. We packed our things and took another taxi into another scary situation full of unknowns.

CHAPTER 14

THE HOTEL INN

When we pulled up to the Ronkonkoma Inn, it was a big, rundown hotel. I was uncomfortable from the moment we pulled into the parking lot. There were people hanging out in front of the building and it was located in a wooded area. As a city girl, this was very unnerving to me. I was not used to this type of environment. I was used to concrete, buildings, and very few trees. When we got there, everyone started coming out of their rooms, checking us out. We could hear people saying, "Who is that lady with those kids?" We were told by the superintendent that the two

97

rooms on the third floor were ours. He gave us keys and gave us all of the rules that we had to follow if we wanted to live there. No hot plates, there was a curfew, and you could not go into anyone's room without their permission, etc. However, no one followed those rules.

The rules of the Ronkonkoma Inn were set by a very big drug dealer who lived there with his girlfriend. We learned that we knew the drug dealer's family and that they lived a couple of towns over from us at one time. Not only did his girlfriend live there, but two of his sisters-in-law lived there.

It was a disgusting place. The next day, we could see the regular activities and the normal state of the hotel. Crack fiends and dopeheads were laying in the hallways. It reminded me of a scene from the 1991 film *New Jack City*. The drug dealer had the place on lock and there were people all over the place.

I will never forget the day when I saw a woman in the hallway of the hotel. She was dancing around in the hallway doing the crackhead fiend dance. I was looking at her in amazement, not knowing what would happen next. I have seen people smoke crack before, and I thought that was what was supposed to happen. She continued to dance and then she took a rubber tie-off and wrapped it around her arm. I was looking at her and could not stop. She had me captivated with her crazy behavior. Once the rubber tie-off was tight enough, she took out a needle and squirted a liquid into the air, and then she shoved the needle into her arm. Within seconds, her eyes rolled to the back of her head and she fell back limp in the hallway. I could not believe what I was seeing. That was the first time I saw someone give themselves heroin, and I knew it was not something I would ever be curious enough to try. It was such an awkward situation because no one even moved. We just kept hanging out in the hallway. It was so weird.

After living in this environment for a couple of months, I started hanging out with one of the chicks who lived in the hotel. She happened to be a sister-in-law of the drug dealer who ran it. She helped me to get into selling crack to the residents of the building. Although the big dealer had the hotel on lock, she would sneak into his room and take the residue left behind after he cut all he was going to sell. The residue

would be enough to resell to the crack heads when

they did not have enough money to buy a good amount

from him, or when they wanted to buy something and

he was not around. We swore them to secrecy and

there is no one more loyal than someone hooked on

crack. They would sell their own mother to ensure they

could get high. More than one source for them to get

the drugs was a win-win for them, so we were safe

with this side hustle. My mother was also instrumental

in making sure we were protected. She had good

relationships with the dealers and the users.

There was a beach right across the street from

the hotel. We used to go there on a regular basis, until

one day a riot broke out at the beach. Some guys from

the hotel were involved with the riot. It escalated in front of the Inn. My older brother was arrested and wrongfully accused, and released.

I always loved the water. It helped me to think and plan. I also had fun with some of the people that lived at the hotel. We used to play Marco Polo in the water and some of the boys would get fresh and touch the girls inappropriately. It never happened to me, though because I was very mean and no one wanted to go there. Neither the boys nor the girls messed with me. They knew I wouldn't tolerate it.

My sister was not so lucky. She tried to make friends with some of the girls, and they were nothing but ghetto gutter-snipes. They were mean-spirited and ignorant. I used to try to talk to her and tell her to stick with me, but she said she didn't just want to be with me all the time.

One night, we could hear my sister screaming. My heart raced and I felt panicked. I didn't know what was going on. I knew she had stayed in one of the girls' rooms that night, but I didn't know what they could have been doing to her. My brothers and I ran to the room we knew she was staying in. At the same time, my sister was running out of the room. She had toothpaste on her face and she reeked of a fishy odor. She kept saying, "They put something on me" and "I'm burning, they put something in my crotch!!"

When we got back to our room, we found that they had put tuna fish and hot sauce in her crotch while she was sleeping. My sister sleeps with her legs agape, so they had access to do this. She was a very hard sleeper too, so I am not surprised that they were able to pull this off. This was their idea of a sick prank. I was enraged. I wanted to go kick their asses but my mother told us to leave it alone. My brother and I still went back to address the girls' room. We looked at them like family, and their prank wasn't funny. I asked them why they did that.

These were the types of crazy things people had to deal with in this ghetto-ass fabulous hotel.

CHAPTER 15

MY QUEEN BELLE BECAME ILL

We left the Ronkonkoma Inn and went to Huntington, where my parents reconciled. We were there for only a few days, when we went to visit my Grandmother and found out that she was very sick. I was chosen to take care of her, so when it was time for my mother and my siblings to leave Nana's, I stayed there with her. I didn't understand why I was chosen, because she had eight children and I was one of her many grandchildren. Little did I know this would finally give me a chance to have a positive relationship within my family.

Nana was diagnosed with a bone disease that deemed her bedridden, so she could not take care of herself. I was wondering how I could possibly help her, what would be required, and if I was capable of giving her the care she needed. I was very apprehensive, but then found out that there was an aide during the day and she primarily just needed my help at night. I felt this was manageable and welcomed the change in the environment.

As time went on, Nana and I forged a wonderful relationship. She was a very spiritual woman and was the mother that I had always yearned for. I would tell her some of my deepest secrets. Nana always told me to love my parents no matter what and learn to forgive and forget.

While I started my first loving relationship with my grandmother in the confines of her home, at the same time I began to become stronger and meaner in the streets. I was a force to be reckoned with. Life was like the movie *New Jack City*; crack was the largest hustle in the game. This is when I met my thug passion. His name was Mark. I was hanging outside of the complex where my grandmother lived. This nice car drove past with some fly ass rims. They were shining as the car rolled up the hill. The driver and I locked eyes and I was hooked. Mark was a tall caramel drink of water. I was instantly attracted to him. He had pretty curly black hair and I have a fetish for curly black hair.

Turns out he was visiting his brother, who was trying to kick it to my aunt at the time. His brother lived across the street from the complex. I heard him say, "What's up sexy?" But I looked at him like he was crazy. I was playing hard to get, but inside I was going crazy! I wanted to get at his sexy ass. At the time, I was selling drugs in the hood and I had just got a job as an exotic dancer at a club in Brooklyn. I was supposed to start next week.

After that day, he would often come through and we would kick it. When my grandmother saw that I was interested in him she told me he was no good for me. He was bad news and I really shouldn't get involved with him. Her forbidding me to talk to him made me want to talk to him even more. He wined and dined me and bought me gifts. I had never been treated so well by a man, and I fell head over heels for him. Whatever he asked me to do, I was down. I became obsessed with him, and he was the air that I breathed.

After being with him for a while I saw that he was a very well-known drug dealer. This did not deter me in any way. As a matter of fact, I was attracted to his thuggish lifestyle. He started taking me on runs with him to purchase large amounts of crack cocaine and schooled me on how to sell drugs and make the most cash.

We were together for a few months, and while I was already in the drug game, I was on another level with Mark. I was addicted to him, and even though I knew I could never be his only woman, I was happy to take whatever he gave me. He had a lot of children, and I also found out later, a lot of other women. But I was willing to settle for whatever I received from him at the time. At this point, I had to use what I got to get what I wanted. He was the hands that fed me. I felt whatever made him happy, I would just do it, so I would keep it 100 with him. Like I said, I learned that he had many other women, but the way I looked at it was, those chicks were not my problem. I was fucking him, not them. What's good. I was a straight savage. I was built like the boys. Hit it, run, never hold any emotion, when you're not given a title in someone's life. It was business. Fuck it, I'm homeless, let's get this money.

CHAPTER 16

MAKE THAT MONEY, DON'T LET IT MAKE YOU

Life was chaotic and the struggle was real. I went for the first time to the strip club in Brooklyn, dealing drugs by day, and an exotic dancer by night. Dancing on the stage was the demonic soul of mine. I had no passion for it and it was not like I was dancing for a man I really loved. It was nasty and degrading, but I really needed the money. Money and anger drove me at the time, and whatever I could do to get it, I did. Nothing was off-limits.

When I got on stage, I just wiggled my hips and stroked my hands on my breasts and popped those thighs open to reveal that fatty toward a crowd of drooling men screaming at me. I downed a couple of shots before getting on stage, so I didn't really care. I grabbed the pole and started grinding and spinning on it. They started shouting, "Diamond, turn that big ass around and drop it like it's hot!"

As I was getting ready to get off stage, the manager said I was responsible for getting a four-drink minimum out of the crowd. She said if I wanted to keep my tips, I would have to crawl the bar counter. This was a way to get drinks purchased quicker. I started crawling the bar and then turned my head toward the mirror. I looked at myself and told the manager I was too big and was uncomfortable crawling the bar. What the hell was I thinking? She leaned over in my face and said, "Do what you have to do!"

My eyes fixated on a heavyweight player in the club. I walked over to him seductively and he said he would buy all four drinks if I danced for him. I did just that, in that order. He said, "Drop that thing like you need to. Make big daddy happy." I did that, then paid my dues for the night.

I met my quota and it was time to go downstairs to the changing room. When I got downstairs, I was cornered by some girls in the club. They threatened me and said if I ever came back to the club and made money in their territory, I would pay. One girl was swirling a razor blade in her mouth and another one was getting jacked up on cocaine. They were ready to fuck me up.

I rushed upstairs and asked the manager for my pay for the night and left, never to return. It was for the best. The club had so many things going on in it—strippers were having sex with men for $30.00, giving blow jobs for $20.00, and handjobs were only $5.00. Although I considered myself a woman who could handle herself in the streets, this was not the life I wanted for myself. I realized that there were things that were off-limits that I would not do.

I decided to go to a trade school to get my nursing certification. Once I received it, I started doing private cases and retail, all while still dealing drugs on the side. By this time, Nana had gotten much worse.

She suffered from mini-strokes and eventually died of

a heart attack. I was devastated.

After Nana died, I started to allow work to

consume me. I was working retail and the nursing

cases. I began to deal with drugs less and less.

Something inside of me wanted something more. I

wanted to do well for myself without worrying about

the legal ramifications. I would work retail 12 hours a

day and take the private nursing cases whenever I

could. I wanted to make money and support myself.

During this time, I was making many bad

choices based off of my past, but I was making money

and would do whatever I needed to do in order to

survive. I continued to sell myself to the man that my father had pimped me out to early in my childhood life. I was ashamed and disgusted with myself for having any sexual encounters with any guy that was dating a family member at the time. I had no feelings. A long time ago, I had become numb; now I was a survivor, and whoever got run over had no face or feelings. I was willing to do anything to stop hustling, dancing, being molested and raped for the rest of my life.

The retail store I worked at sold all-occasion gowns as well as wedding dresses. I gained a sort of second family in the retail store. We all got along and the staff was very diverse. Outside of the owners, it was a great place to work. The owners were racist assholes. We had a good time at work, goofing off,

talking, and some of the girls would model the dresses

in a funny way and have everybody cracking up.

Sometimes I wished I could wear the dress, but they

were all for skinny model types. I was a plus-sized girl

and there was no way I was fitting into those gowns.

I found that I was very self-conscious about the

way I looked, because I still had that feeling that I did

not deserve compliments and I did not like them. I

always viewed it as bait to get something else. It just

never entered my mind that someone could actually

admire me from a respectable place.

I worked at the retail store for four years. The

owner would move the black people around in the

store in a segregated way. He did not want us mixing. In spite of his racist practices, we were all very close. It did not matter what he thought. That was his belief and I didn't give a shit. The pay was weekly and it was convenient for me. I liked the fact that I could look forward to having money in my pocket every Friday.

The security guard at the store and I had a thing for each other. We would flirt and mess around, and we would do things like sneaking up to the lunchroom to grab a kiss, or we would meet up after work to go to his house in the city. The shower scenes were off the chain. He would press my face against the shower walls with water running down my face, making sweet love to me. Giving me back shots like a pro. His freaky sex was such a turn on for me, it would make my water flow. In the shower I received 100 percent

enjoyment. I loved it! However, when we had sex in

bed I had difficulty enjoying it as much. I would have

flashbacks of the molesters and the rapists. There was

one time we were in the bed making love and he

grabbed my hips and laid into me as we both exhaled

and released the juices from our bodies. He relaxed his

head on my breast as I caressed every curl on his head.

We had sex through the night then returned to work

the next day.

But there was something I was hiding from my

boo. I could not tell him how good it felt. I just could

not bring myself to do it. I don't know why. I also had

the demons that would enter my mind when we had

sex that I could never reveal to him. These demons

would rob me of my ecstasy. This really pissed me off because this man gave me every sensation I could have ever wanted, emotionally and sexually.

CHAPTER 17

MAKING A DIFFERENCE IN THE COMMUNITY

If you purchased a 50 slab, you would make $100.00 cash after cutting it into little squares and selling them for $20.00 a piece. I was determined not to allow the pain of my past to keep me away from the happiness I knew I deserved. Crack cocaine begin to destroy many families. It was the highest market drug in the street at that time. It also incarcerated half of the men in the black communities, who weren't getting set up by the police or wrongfully accused by jurisdictions, or getting shot up by the OG from the hood over territory. The whole town was the freaks come out at night.

My dad couldn't beat his drug habit. He ended up in a diabetic coma and died shortly after; his body couldn't fight off the infection. Although my father resented me, when it was time for his burial, my oldest brothers did what they could to contribute and empty my whole savings for the funeral. He was our dad and it was between him and God how he treated his children.

I worked as a CNA for four years and I continued to work in the retail industry, but I was getting fed up with the racist ways of the owners. The owners were Jewish and very racist. I was not going to settle and accept bad treatment because of the color of my skin.

It was also during this time I was still seeing the drug dealer off and on. One day I was at work and felt a sharp pain and thought I had pulled something. I went to the hospital where, to my surprise, I found out I was pregnant with twins. It was an ectopic pregnancy and I eventually lost the babies. I felt all alone because the dude and I were just friends with benefits. The doctors also told me the devastating news that I would never be able to have children because one of the twins burst a tube in my stomach.

It was also during this time that I ran into a community service worker, Ms. Bailey, who I knew from my childhood struggles. She would help my mother with community resources. She told me that the new childcare center that opened up in the community was looking for teachers and she encouraged me to apply, telling me that I was always good with children. I went for an interview. I was offered a job as a toddler teacher. I was so excited that I finally found something that I really enjoyed doing. Working with the children gave me a newfound purpose. I began to become so passionate about my job and the difference that I was making, not only in the lives of the children, but also in the lives of the parents.

Over the years, I worked my way from being a toddler teacher to presently being the assistant director.

I'm forever grateful for the chance that the owner gave me to grow and mature. The owner gave me the opportunity, but Miss Tammy and Miss Brenda taught me the business side of childcare, and all three of them have become more than just coworkers. I can call them role models, and most of all my friends and some of my biggest supporters. The owner of the facility is the Godmother of one of my sons. Ms. Tammy is the Godmother to my other son.

Over the years, we have developed a relationship far deeper than co-workers; she is a mother figure and she understands me better than most people. She saw the potential in me before I did, and she pushed me to be a better version of me. I have shared things with her that I have never shared with anyone else. We share a deep-rooted relationship and she has been a large part of my healing process. She welcomed me into her family and never judged me for my past. She encouraged me to allow that little rejected girl that lived inside of me to grow up into the woman that I am today and she will also tell me the truth. She also helped me to understand that my mother/father had a lot of unresolved issues and that she did the best she could with the hand that life dealt her and that in order for me to be free mentally, it was necessary for me to forgive her and release all the bitterness that I felt towards my mother all these years, and I am happy that I was able to before my mother died.

I have been working since I was nine years old, so I have developed a work ethic that many do not understand; therefore one of my hardest struggles is dealing with women and their different attitudes and personalities. I had never really developed relationships with many women since all of my life I have been a tomboy, and I get along better with men than I do with women. Some women are so petty and want to be in competition with one another. They are gossipers and backbiters and they will stab you in your back, quick, fast, and in a hurry. So at the job, I've learned if women don't like me, stay in my lane. If they are in their feelings about me, I don't care. I have a job to do.

I didn't come looking for friends, but to provide a safe haven for the children in my community. I live where I work, so it's much more than a job for me. It's my purpose to make sure they are safe. There was no one to save me, so I have to be a Savior to each and every child that walks through that door.

CHAPTER 18

HAVING STRONG FAITH TO SURVIVE

You can recognize survivors of abuse by their courage. When silence is so very inviting, they step forward and share their truth so others know they aren't alone. ~ Jeanne McElvaney

Sometimes it is not an outside force that is destroying us, but sometimes it is us. Sometimes life has beaten us down so bad, and as women, we have endured a great deal. We deal with it. Daddy left, so we have daddy issues, low self-confidence, low self-esteem, unforgiveness, and brokenness. As we become

129

wives and mothers, our past can often hinder our future. We feel that we are unworthy to be in love and that we will never truly be whole because we feel so broken.

At this point in my life, I felt like I would never experience true love and happiness. Learning to become a woman has been a difficult path for me. I am a good person. I can overcome what happened to me by keeping myself in check. Like all women, I have my doubts and my insecurities, but the depths of how far they went travel back to my childhood. I wasn't able to look into the mirror. I hated all men. I tortured myself mentally and physically. I destroyed myself because I didn't feel worthy, and the biggest issue I had was with my inability to say no. It wasn't until my recent past, during my journey of self-discovery and healing, that I learned in the subsidy of being able to say no when I need to and when I want to. Realizing that served as an initiative to start doing better for myself, because one of the greatest lessons I've learned is it's not just learning how to say no, but being able to say yes to me.

I was mad at the girl in the mirror and that's why I resisted her. I didn't want to do anything my reflection was about. I was ashamed, and because of my fears from the threats I received from those who continued to hurt me, I continued to feel humiliation. I believed that I was ugly and not worthy of anybody, and what bothered me the most was that it still upset me at times. I get upset at myself for not being the person I am now. I want to be able to make a difference in my present, so

I can protect myself from my past experiences. I would often wish that I were stronger and able to fight harder.

The hardest fight of my life was not with the outside world, or even with my abuser, but my hardest battle is with the reflection I see in the mirror. I had to come to the conclusion that it was not my fault. It was time to stop blaming the victim. It was time for me to transition from victim to victory. I am victorious despite all that I have gone through. I am still here. I am a survivor.

I slowly began to transform into the woman that I am today. I am not going to lie; it wasn't easy, but it was necessary for me to discover the woman that God designed me to be. I am fearfully and wonderfully made. Every day is a new opportunity for me to look at myself to discover a new way of reminding myself of the reasons why I love me. I am continually finding new ways to meet and greet the new, confident woman that I am becoming. I am still a work in progress because there are still times when I feel insecure and fearful. I am scared that the personalities that I created to cope with my past will rear their ugly head as they clash to stop me from being me. I have guarded my heart for so many years, it is hard for me to accept the love of those around me. I know that I deserve to be loved, but I am scared of putting down my guard and being hurt again. After all, that had been my reality for many years; therefore I had to fight to stop it from holding my future hostage.

CHAPTER 19

MEETING MY FOREVER FRIEND/HUSBAND

One of my life-defining moments was twenty years ago when I met Tyrese, a fine Jamaican man. I wasn't interested in his looks, but he was a gentleman who was very cocky and confident in himself. He is now my husband. He was a contractor and owned his own business. When we first met, it was strictly for business. My baby brother Terrance would have temper tantrums and would punch holes in the wall. Well, I really shouldn't say it was all business, because I was interested in this brother, but the plan to get close to him was to hire him to fix the holes my brother had put in the wall, and we couldn't call the landlord about the damages done to the property. I got him to come to my house because I needed a handyman.

I finally made the phone call that would eventually change my life. One of my coworkers encouraged me to call him. She said he fixes things, and you need something fixed, what a perfect combination. When I first met him, I was renting a three-bedroom apartment with my mother and younger brother. He came over and fixed the damage, and I found myself growing more attracted to him and there was an undeniable chemistry that was hitting me like a bolt of lightning. I had never felt like this. We flirted with each other, but it didn't happen the way I thought it would. The flame never turned into a fire, so I continued working at the daycare center and living the single life.

I was getting frustrated with my living situation because I was used to having my own apartment, but my mother's health was failing, and my younger brother was not capable of taking care of my mom alone. So once again I sacrificed my own happiness for someone who seemingly didn't give a damn about me or the sacrifice I was making. But no matter what hell she put me through, she was still my mother.

I was living life and had basically put Tyrese out of my mind, but as fate would have it, I ran into him again and things started happening fast. Within a month of us dating, we began to get physical. We had kissed before, but on this particular night we were at my place, lying in bed kissing. It was dark.

After kissing and foreplay, I felt him raise himself up to get on top of me, but as soon as he did, I no longer just saw him, but images of the person who had molested me for nine years was the face that I saw on top of me; it was no longer Tyrese's face. Both of their faces were flashing back and forth until I could no longer see Tyrese, only the image that haunted me. I began to attack him by pushing and kicking him off of me. All I could envision was that I was being attacked again and I called Tyrese by this other man's name. As it would be expected, Tyrese asked me why I did that, and why I was acting so violently against him.

137

I had this man asking me questions as I was simultaneously trying to figure it out at the same time. I was ashamed and confused as all of these feelings I had suppressed for so many years started to overtake me. I had all of these memories that were flashing in my mind. I tried to stop the flashbacks but those horrible memories were like a rerun playing over and over again. Tyrese told me that something had to have happened in my life for me to be reacting this way.

Over time, it was like he was reading me, while I was denying myself. He told me I should talk to someone about what was going on with me. My heart started to open up. I'd had boyfriends in the past, or at least friends with benefits. What I now realize was that I'd never allowed any of them in my heart because of all those years I'd hated men. This was the first man that I tried to put my guard down with, but I still had the residue from my past all over me. My heart wanted to let him in and allow him to know the real me, but being in my head was standing in the way. I just didn't know how this would be possible. There were times when I didn't even know myself. There was so much of my past that I blocked and locked away. I wanted to let my guard down and share my deepest emotions with him, but this was a new relationship and I didn't want him to see me as damaged goods. What I did know was that he wasn't like those other jokers I was used to being with. I could really see a future with him. Therefore, I wanted to be better. I knew I wanted to be better, but I didn't know where to start.

The first year of our relationship was mentally difficult, because I was trying to work through my own issues so that I could be with him. Looking back on it, I was faking my emotions throughout the beginning of our relationship. I was trying to be what I thought I was supposed to be, not realizing that I was enough. I never thought that I was worthy of the life that I so desired. I was stuck in the way that the old Diamond thought and carried on, and I didn't care because I separated my emotions based on how I knew how to deal with them. Sex and pain had become my way of life.

When he started fooling around with other women on me, people were gossiping about him, but what they didn't know is that I was telling him to go and f*** someone else because I wasn't going to f*** him. I was stubborn and eventually had to apologize because I was cold-hearted and really f***** up. It took me awhile to realize I was afraid of him leaving me, so I was trying to push him away. I needed to feel like I was in control of my feelings. For him to leave me, that would be like him proving to me that I wasn't good enough.

He had me experience feelings that were new to me. I was afraid that I would trust him with my heart and he would break it like everyone that I ever cared about had done in the past. I was afraid of the good things happening to me, as I was afraid of the bad things happening to me again.

I was fortunate that he was patient, and he is the man that was able to be the strength that I needed to help me through this. His way of being patient was being persistent with me. Tyrese became the most reliable person I knew in my life. Always being there, always showing up, even when he felt he shouldn't has helped my everyday struggle of surpassing my past. He was learning how to give me compliments even when I denied them. I would continuously shut him down when he would come at me sexually. I thought his ideas and opinions of me were just a way to use me and manipulate me. He would, and still up to this day, Tyrese initiates our intimate time, unless I have a drink or two. To this day, he tells me I need to open up and share my thoughts and feelings with him.

As I stated before, Tyrese and my two sons are the main reasons why I am finally sharing my truths with the world. I am a very private person who had been conditioned to keep what happened in the house, in the house, but in order for me to be mentally okay for—first of all—me, then my husband and children. If I don't take care of Diamond, I will never be able to have healthy relationships with those that matter most. But my exodus from my past wasn't an easy journey and I still haven't totally arrived.

CHAPTER 20

STARTING OUR NEW FAMILY

When I started dating Tyrese, I also inherited a daughter who I affectionately called 'Stink.' It was difficult because, at that time in my life, I didn't want kids. I didn't feel like I was emotionally available the way kids need parents to be full-time. It's ironic because at the time I met Tyrese and his daughter, I was a daycare provider and great with kids, but that was from 9:00 to 5:00. To be a parent full-time, it's something I wasn't ready for, but I learned to embrace my baby girl Stink. She put me in a more responsible state. I didn't take to her for a long time. I was

144

struggling with feelings of having to take care of this little girl because I was in a relationship with her father, but to this day I regret the pain from my past life that stopped me from loving her the way a little girl needs to be loved. I wish that we could have done more mother/daughter events.

Tyrese and Stink were the first two people who taught me what unconditional love was. As hard as I was fighting to push him away, the harder Tyrese was fighting to prove his love for me. It was difficult for him to chisel through the wall I had built around my heart, but he never gave up on me. As I continually state, he is a large part of why I am writing this book. He didn't judge me for my past, but he wanted me to be totally healed so I could realize that what happened wasn't my fault. It was the hand I was dealt and that was the hand that I played, but it was time for the game to be over.

For many years, I hid behind many masks or personalities. It was time for healing, but healing is a continuing process. It is hard for you to love someone when you don't love yourself. It is even harder for someone to love you.

CHAPTER 21

GIVING BIRTH TO TWO KINGS

In 2003, I had my first son and shortly after, we got married while I was pregnant with my second son in 2005. I love my kids and there isn't anything I wouldn't do to protect them, even if I believe it's from me. I didn't want to get close to my kids, because I didn't want to feel like I didn't love them. I was finally ready for a real relationship, or at least at that point where I thought I was ready, but I didn't realize that I still had a great deal of healing to do. But I was finally in a relationship with a man that values me and didn't just see me as a sex toy like the previous relationships that I had been in all of my life. A small part of me was willing to take a risk on life.

We had begun to spend a lot of time together, which was actually the beginning of why I'm writing the story of my life. That was the beginning of me coping with me using sex against him. At this point, I had opened up an ugly can of worms, and rightly so, he was looking for answers. I really couldn't explain what I was going through because I had suppressed my past for so long and hid behind a façade. But this incident made me realize there were some things I had to face and to get help, or my past would continue to hold me prisoner.

At the same time that I began to have recurring dreams and nightmares, my relationship with Tyrese was getting stronger, and for the first time, I was really falling in love and we began to live together. It was during the same time that he was going to Family Court, fighting for full custody of his daughter. So instantaneously, I had a new relationship and a ready-made family. I had my bonus five-year-old little girl. For the first time, I felt like a part of a happy family. I continued to work at the daycare and to bring my new bundle of joy to work with me every day.

We started living together for a couple of years and I became pregnant, but I didn't know at the time I was pregnant. Tyrese told me that I was pregnant, but I told him that that was impossible, because first of all I was taking a pill, and the doctor had told me that I would never be able to have children. All of my life my cycle was irregular and it continued to be irregular throughout my pregnancy. My body began to change when I was five months pregnant.

When my son was born, it was one of the happiest and saddest days of my life. I really had no idea what to do with this colicky, crying baby. To make matters worse, I was suffering from postpartum depression and I started rejecting my baby and not establishing a healthy, nurturing relationship between a mother and their baby.

It was also during this time there started to be trouble in paradise, and our happy home was no longer a happy place, but a place of misery. I was working long hours and accusing him of being with other women. I was basically giving him the time to do what he wanted. I started to see other women's items like hair clips in my car that didn't belong to me. I questioned him about these things and he made me appear like I was the crazy one. He started staying out later and making excuses, but one day he could no longer deny the truth. The side chick thought it was a good idea to make an appearance at my door and to explain to me all about their relationship and how she had been sleeping with him for months. To add fuel to the fire, not only was he cheating on me with her, but he had slept with her in our apartment. She was able to describe my entire apartment, including my bedroom, to me. There was no way that he could lie his way out of this one. I packed up my son and I moved out of the apartment.

Tyrese tried over and over again to apologize and said he was sorry for all the hurt and pain that he caused, but he still wanted us to be a family. I eventually forgave him and we tried to move on because my son was yearning for his father, and the truth be told, I still love him.

As we were trying to work things out, the road was still bumpy. At my son's first birthday party, all hell broke out. An argument broke out between his family and my family. He had the audacity to have this other chick that he had been sleeping with for three years while the both of us were still in a relationship, at my son's birthday party. I shortly found out that she was also pregnant. I was standing there looking like a total fool in front of my family and friends. At that point, our family was divided.

He took his daughter and moved out, and I kept our son with me. This made me go back into my shell and I was having a very difficult time. For the first time, I let my guard down and let someone in, and he broke my heart, shattering it into pieces.

One night, sitting outside of my apartment, I began hyperventilating and having an anxiety attack. My son was in the back seat. Luckily for me, I was on the phone with my boss who rushed to my apartment. By the time she arrived, I was throwing up and couldn't stop. She insisted that I go to the hospital. After being poked and prodded, they discovered that I

was pregnant with baby number two, who was
conceived during makeup sex.

I told Tyrese that I wasn't having another baby
out of wedlock. I told him that we needed to go to
marriage counseling. We got married while I was eight
months pregnant, moved out of the apartment, and
bought our first home. We went from being a family of
three to a family of five. Financially, things were
getting very tight and we were both working so hard at
making ends meet that we had very little time to work
on our relationship. We were struggling to make our
relationship work and to salvage the love that we had
left, because now we had a great deal invested in our
marriage. We had a home and three children
depending on us.

I was at this point struggling with trust issues. I was trying to work on my marriage, but I didn't trust him anymore. It wasn't all of his fault. I have to bear some of the blame. I lacked the skills to communicate my feelings and inside of sharing my pain with him, I shut him off, including refusing to have intimate relations with him.

I was sharing bits and pieces of my past with my supervisor. God had sent great people in my life that understood the hold that my past had on me.

CHAPTER 22

BEAUTY FOR MY ASHES

I had suffered so many years of sexual abuse, physical and mental abuse. I shared my story to empower myself and others like me who, for years, have suffered in silence. You can recover from your past and childhood trauma. The road to recovery is difficult and painful. You are able to regain control of your life. The first thing that you have to do is forgive yourself because it is not your fault. Sexual abuse is common in America. According to the CDC, 1 out of every 5 women will be sexually abused in their life. The trauma of being sexually abused has lingering effects in your life. It can leave you shattered, broken, and angry.

I was scared and ashamed. I was plagued with flashbacks, bad dreams, and horrible memories. It was at an early age that I learned that the world is not a safe place. I learned that I could not trust anyone, not even myself. I would often blame my parents and most of all blamed myself. I felt like no one would ever really love me because I was worthless and damaged goods.

I had suppressed what had happened to me for many years. I had to first admit what happened. I had to tell someone what I endured in my childhood. This was extremely difficult for me because inside I felt so, so dirty, and for years my family had convinced me that this was our dirty little secret. We didn't want people to know how dysfunctional we really were.

When I reached adulthood, people would say, "That happened so long ago. Why do you want to start trouble and relive the past?" I had to finally decide it was time for me to do what was best for me. I had spent too many years avoiding my feelings and memories in order to just be able to get by on a daily basis. I also felt hopeless. I had given up all hope years ago.

The abuse was still affecting me in a major way. It showed up in my relationships, and certain things would trigger negative reactions in me and would show in how I handled my emotions. I was having

sexual and emotional issues that were not getting any

better over the years. The new relationships I was in

had me all in my feelings that was making me aware

of my past experiences. As I began to deal with my

issues, I found out I was not alone. Many children

have suffered sexual abuse. Truth be told, I wasn't the

only one in my family, but they have to take their own

path to recovery.

My truth is that I was a victim of sexual abuse,

starting at the age of four until adulthood. Sexual

abuse is when a person is forced into a sexual act

without their consent. One of the hardest things for me

to do is to trust people, because my trusting nature was

destroyed at an early age. I was taught that I had to

keep my abuse hidden in order to protect my family. I was often in disbelief and sometimes in denial about what I suffered as a child. As a child, I escaped from reality and fabricated my own reality, and I would pretend to be a superhero. I was taught to put other's needs before my own needs. I allowed myself to be taken advantage of so many times, I often didn't realize that I have the right and the ability to take control of my own life. I was often angry. I even thought of ways I could kill all of those people who had taken advantage of me in my past. I was angry with myself because I thought maybe I could have fought harder. I was angry with my parents because they didn't protect me. I was angry with my mother because she blamed me. I suffered a deep depression silently. The sexual abuse robbed me of the ability to have healthy sexual relationships. I hated my body and when men would compliment me, especially bring attention to my big behind, I would retreat back into my shell.

As my memories of my sexual abuse started to resurface, I went from being an emotionless, sexual person, to being totally shut down sexually. Every time Tyrese tried to touch me, I didn't want to be touched.

I had to realize that I was not a victim, but I was an overcomer. I was a survivor. It was because of my past, I am a strong woman. I am more than what happened to me. I was no longer a victim. I had no control over the things that happened to me in the past, but I have control over whether or not I would allow my past to make me bitter or better. This time I had to choose to get better. My family was depending on me to get better, to stop the generational curses and to let the skeletons fall out of the closet.

I did seek help for a while, while this was happening to me because I was a frightened little girl, but now I am a woman, but that little girl still lives inside of me. For many years, I tried to deal with the trauma on my own. The first time I told someone, they didn't believe me and told me if it did happen, it was because I was a little slut.

When I shared my story with my director, who has become more than just a supervisor and coworker, she is family; she was the first one that validated my feelings. She provided me with a safe haven where I could share my thoughts and my truths. I didn't have to worry about her telling my business because everything was confidential. She told me that my feelings mattered and were important. She also reassured me that it was not my fault. She reassured me that there were men out there who could be trusted. She encouraged me to talk eventually about my abuse and my many abusers. I had a lot of work to do to get healthy and it was a long, hard process because there was so much leftover residue that I had from my childhood, but I finally had the strength to rise out of the ashes to rise above my circumstances. I had to rise up from victim to victor.

I took the time to mourn the betrayal that I faced from people in my life. I had to mourn what could have been if my childhood weren't snatched away from me. I grieved all the things, people, and places that I have lost over the years. I buried my pain because, if I didn't bury it, I would never get over it. I had to take off the bandage, because under the bandage was rotting and stinking. It was time for me to acknowledge my past, but I could no longer have it define who I am now. My past shaped who I am today. I did not choose the circumstances I was born into. You cannot choose your family.

I had to make a list of those things that triggered me. One of my main triggers is the smell of saliva because my abuser would spit on my genitals to make it easier for him to penetrate me. The smell of urine is also a trigger because during those horrendous acts of abuse I would urinate on myself, hoping that would turn him off. I also don't like kissing and I have a problem initiating intimacy. I will fantasize about different sexual positions and allow myself to experience sexual freedom. My husband is so patient and understanding, and he doesn't force me to do anything that I am not emotionally able to do.

CHAPTER 23

MOMMY AND DADDY DEAREST

One of the main steps in my healing process was to deal with my relationship with my mother and father. Over the years, I hated my parents because I felt that they failed as parents because they failed to protect me from the ugliness of the world. They allowed my childhood to be taken from me. As I shared my story with my older brother, he felt that if he had known, he would have killed him, but I told him it wasn't his responsibility to protect me, it was our parents that dropped the ball. My mother would blame me for the abuse, making allegations that I was just hot tailed and too grown, which was a lie that she told herself to rationalize her actions.

She acted for most of my life like she really hated me. I don't even think that she knew me as Diamond, because she referred to me as a bitch. I can give her credit for making me the woman that I am. I learned at an early age how to hustle and take care of myself. She taught me how to make a dollar out of fifteen cents. They taught me how to work hard, because if you don't work, you don't eat.

I often wish my relationship with my parents would have been different, but it was what it was. They never had the chance to see me grown up. It saddens me to see other people with strong mother/daughter or father/daughter relationships, because I never had it. My supervisor who I affectionately now call "mom" said, "I could never wear your mom's shoes but I can show you that maternal love that a mother and daughter should have."

One of the most important lessons that my supervisor taught me was not to hold my mom accountable to a certain extent, because she did the best that she could with the knowledge that she had. She was also a victim, but one that never took the opportunity to heal, so hurt people hurt other people. They bleed on those who did not cause the injury because they are incapable of unconditional love.

It's funny that before my mom passed away, I would still dream about us having a fairytale relationship. I would buy a big house with a separate apartment for her and I would take care of her and she would finally love me as a mother should love her daughter. We never reached that point in our relationship, but I forgave her for all of her years of physical, emotional, and mental abuse.

I forgive my mother for waking up out of being in a diabetic coma, and when she was able to speak when they removed the tube out of her mouth, she said to me, "Why did you save me bitch? Nobody ask for your fucking help."

I looked at her and told her she should be careful. She is going to reap what she sows, how she is treating her own daughter.

I finally realized that by me holding onto all of that bitterness and pain was not healthy for me. Forgiveness is an easy word to say, but a difficult action to carry out. It hurt me that my mother rejected me. I was always trying to find the reason why, out of all of her children, she hated me the most.

Childhood trauma has such an effect on people's lives. Emotionally, I desperately tried to avoid all of those painful thoughts and memories. I tried mental detours when certain thoughts would enter my head; I would block them. I would avoid conversations and situations that would remind me of my past.

There were so many negative things that I had suppressed. I attempted to bury my pain. I tried to dig a hole so deep and cover up all of the pain and misery from my past. But no matter how deep the hole was, my pain and hurt found its way out and it showed up by the way I behaved. It showed up in my relationships and how I dealt with people. My lack of faith and trust in people. I had to deal with the root of my problem, the root of my bitterness. I had to make the connection between my past and my future.

The one thing I realize is that I have not forgiven the monster who caused me all of this pain. It is still raw and painful. I realize that this is a process and I have to be transparent and honest. I have not gotten to that point in my recovery that I am able to forgive him. I understand that my forgiving him is not for him, but it's for me and my wellbeing. I feel that he will never change and continue in his monstrous ways until he dies or someone has the courage to speak up before the statute of limitations are up.

CHAPTER 24

NO CHILD LEFT BEHIND

Statistics have shown that a new case of sexual abuse is reported every nine minutes in America. Sexual abuse is not limited to inappropriate sexual activity, but it includes showing or taking pictures and exposing yourself to a child. I know from my own experiences the impact that sexual abuse can have on their quality of life and even their physical development. It will have an impact on the victim.

One of the first steps in preventing sexual abuse is to know the signs. It is not easy to spot a child that is being victimized, because the predator does a good job of covering up his or her tracks, because remember women can also be predators. There are some physical signs that you can look out for. If the child gets a sexually transmitted disease. If you notice unusual bruises or blood on the child's genital area. They might also demonstrate behavioral signs such as inappropriate sexual behavior. They might start bedwetting; that was one of my defense mechanisms. I started wetting the bed, thinking that would deter my abuser. They will often not want to be left alone with the predator. They might experience emotional signs, such as having nightmares, anxiety, and panic attacks.

It is hard to keep children safe because it is often people who you know, not strangers, that victimize your child. It's important that you watch the way adults interact with your child, because they start grooming the child for sexual abuse even before the actual abuse starts. As a parent, it's imperative that you pay attention to any person that is taking an interest in your child. They gain your child's trust by paying special attention to them. They will buy them gifts and convince them that they are the only one that loves and understands them. These predators will usually prey on children who have low self-esteem and are vulnerable.

Once the abuse begins, they threaten them that they will kill them or their family. They will also tell them that nobody will believe them and if they do, they are the ones who are going to get into trouble because they really wanted them to do it.

As a parent, if you notice someone paying unusual attention to your child, intervene quickly. Establish a relationship with your child so they're not afraid to share anything with you. Teach them at a young age that keeping secrets, especially secrets that harm someone, is not good. Also, begin to teach them about 'good touch' and 'bad touch' as early as they can understand. It is also important that you teach them the real names of their body parts. A vagina is a vagina, a penis is a penis.

If you are in the childcare field, remember you are a mandated reporter, and if you see something, say something. It is also important to understand that childhood sexual abuse goes across all socioeconomic and cultural backgrounds. You can't just look at someone and say that person doesn't look like a child abuser. In the news, we have seen judges, doctors, and lawyers that have abused kids.

Some children that are being abused will show symptoms and others will not. Some of the signs that you can look out for is if a child has become withdrawn inside. The child might also stop wetting the bed and having nightmares. They might become aggressive and show inappropriate sexual behaviors.

It's important to understand that if you notice something does seem suspicious, you do not have to prove something is wrong; you make the call and the authorities will do the investigation. By speaking up, you'll be saving a child from a lifetime of pain and suffering. As adults, it is our job to do what is in the best interest of the child. That's one of the reasons I am in the childcare field. I want to make sure that every child that I come into contact with knows that I am a safe haven and I will always be there for them. Today, you can make the pledge that no child will become a victim on your watch.

CHAPTER 25

RESOURCES

So often, survivors have had their experiences

denied, trivialized, or distorted. Writing is an

important avenue for healing because it gives you the

opportunity to define your own reality. You can say:

This did happen to me. It was that bad. It was the fault

& responsibility of the adult. I was—and am—innocent

~ Ellen Bass

New York State Office of Family and Children Services:
Toll-Free: (800) 342-3720
TDD: (800) 369-2437
Local (toll): (518) 474-8740
https://ocfs.ny.gov/main/cps/Default.asp

Childhood National Abuse Hotline:
Call or text 1.800.4.A.CHILD (1.800.422.4453).
Professional crisis counselors are available 24 hours a
day, 7 days a week, in over 170 languages. All calls
are confidential. The hotline offers crisis intervention,
information, and referrals to thousands of emergency,
social service, and support resources.

CHAPTER 26

REFLECTIONS

1. Are you a victim of childhood sexual abuse?

2. Have you shared your story with anyone?

3. If you did, did they believe you?

4. If you didn't, how has the childhood trauma affected your relationships with significant others and your family?

5. Can you relate to Diamond's story?

6. How did her relationship with her mother affect her life?

7. Do you think she will ever be able to forgive her abusers?

Made in the USA
Middletown, DE
02 August 2020